BARRIER FREE REAL ESTATE

REAL ESTATE

Achieving Freedom at Home

2nd Edition

Jeffrey Kerr

Foreword by David Onley

Cover design by Donna Chabot

Interior design by Andy Meaden / meadencreative.com

Author Contact: info@AccessibleHomeFinder.com

Author Website: www.AccessibleHomeFinder.com

ISBN 978-1-989203-09-5

Published by Three Birds Press www.ThreeBirdsPress.com

Disclaimer

This book is not intended as a substitute for the advice of physicians, occupational therapists, health care professionals, and licenced contractors. The reader should consult with their health care team in matters related to health and mobility and consult with licenced contractors regarding home renovations.

References are provided for informational purposes only and do not constitute endorsement of any product, person, services or website. The information and website links in this book are current at the time of publishing and may need to be updated in the future.

Neither the author nor publisher has received any remuneration for mentioning the products, people, services or websites in this book.

This book in not indented to solicit properties already under contract.

The reader is encouraged to do their own research to find solutions that work for them. The author's opinions are his own.

CONTENTS

Some individuals who function well in a barrier-free environment can find themselves disabled by design.

"Aging in place" is the notion of planning ahead to ensure you can safely and independently live in your own home for as long as you want.

Two key features of a barrier-free entrance include an accessible path of travel and a low or zero-threshold doorway.

The expression "opening doors" can mean creating opportunities; it can also refer to physically opening a door. This chapter is about both, since having a door open automatically for you can create a lot of opportunities at home.

A well-designed bathroom can often be the difference between independence and dependence at home.

Good design is the foundation of an efficient and accessible kitchen that maximizes independence and convenience.

FOREWORD

By Hon. David C. Onley. CM, OOnt.

Lieutenant Governor of Ontario, 2007 to 2014.

Drawing upon almost 22 years in the Real Estate field, Jeffrey Kerr has developed a deserved reputation as an expert in helping clients find or sell accessible housing. The first edition of *Achieving Freedom At Home*, written in 2016, became the instant "go-to" book for persons with disabilities to find the kind of information necessary to make informed decisions.

Now, in the midst of the Covid-19 pandemic, special challenges face persons with disabilities, challenges that are met with this excellent Second Edition of *Achieving Freedom At Home*, a compendium of information which stands alone as the single most important resource a disabled person can acquire before venturing into the often daunting world of finding accessible housing.

Right from the start, Kerr addresses issues facing persons with disabilities, specifically that individuals who function well in a barrier-free environment can find themselves disabled by the very design of the home they wish to buy.

From there he confronts the reality faced by many "boomers" aging in place.

Like the top-notch broker he is, Kerr takes the reader on a mental guided tour from the Entrance to Opening Doors to Bathroom Solutions, to Efficient and Accessible Kitchens. Each stop along the way presents the reader with fresh insights on what to look for to achieve accessible living.

Need information on the ideal home office? Wondering if there's such a thing as an affordable elevator lift device to make a two-story home a realistic option for the mobility challenged? Curious about the latest in Technology, Assistive Devices, and Research? Concerned about having a "visitable home" so that those with disabilities can be guests? Each of these issues are addressed thoroughly and with keen insight.

If you are familiar with experts in the industry like Randy Sora, Accessibility Design/Management Consultant at EZaccess Inc., or Yves Trottier of Simple Freedom Design, you will find their advice to be both wise and easily understood. If you've not heard of them before, you will be glad to discover their insights.

Whether it's the latest in Technology, Lighting, Furniture, or Assistive Devices, Jeffrey Kerr's *Achieving Freedom at Home* is an easily read and understood resource for any person with a disability searching for the knowledge and insights to guide them into an accessible place they can proudly call home.

In a world with precious little information on accessible housing, I find *Achieving Freedom At Home* an invaluable resource for buyer and seller alike and thank Jeffrey for his major contribution to improving the lives of persons with disabilities.

Jeffrey Kerr and David Onley, 2014

INTRODUCTION

For over 21 years I've been a REALTOR® with RE/MAX Unique Inc. in Toronto. During that time I have developed a very specific real estate specialization – helping clients buy and sell barrier-free, wheelchair accessible homes, both houses and condominiums.

In 2016, I wrote the first edition of this book. And now, four years later, at the peak of the COVID 19 pandemic, I felt it was important to write the second edition.

With everything around us changing day by day, Achieving Freedom At Home is now more relevant than ever.

The pandemic has demonstrated the value and importance of having a safe and comfortable home you can live, work, and thrive in. This is especially true for the over 6 million Canadians who have a disability and for the 23% of Canadians who will be over the age of 65 by the year 2030. If you or someone you know is included in one of these categories, then this book is written for you.

My Story

My mom was accredited by the University of Toronto as both a physiotherapist and occupational therapist. She worked for many years at Lyndhurst Hospital which is now part of Toronto Rehab. My aunt had multiple sclerosis and used a wheelchair for mobility.

Growing up with these two strong influences in my life, I learned a lot about accessibility at a very young age. Fast forward to the mid '90s: I started building houses and then earned my real estate licence in 1999 to sell the houses I was building.

My decision to focus on barrier-free homes came as a direct result of a preconstruction condo that my aunt and uncle purchased in the late '90s. The condo was marketed as wheelchair accessible with a custom kitchen, bathroom, and roll-out balcony. By the time the condo was ready for occupancy in 2004, my uncle had passed on and I was with my aunt as she rolled through the front door.

She knew very quickly that she could not live independently in that condo. Although the bathroom had a spacious roll-in shower and she could roll out to the balcony, the kitchen layout was a disaster. The counter heights were disjointed, the sink was crammed into the corner, and the wall oven controls were not reachable. My aunt handed me the keys and asked me to sell the condo.

Aunt Jeane with Jeffrey's kids in 2006

I soon realized that no one in the Greater Toronto Area specialized in helping people with disabilities buy and sell homes. I chose to fill that need and now I use my construction knowledge and my real estate expertise to specialize in helping clients buy and sell barrier-free homes.

I earned my real estate licence in 1999 and my broker's licence in 2007. I have both the Senior Real Estate Specialist (SRES) and Accredited Senior Agent (ASA) designations. Since 2013 I have been a regular columnist in Spinal Cord Injury Ontario's Outspoken! and *Community* magazines. I have been a presenter for both the March of Dimes and the Ontario Real Estate Association on the topic of barrier-free real estate. The CBC, *Globe and Mail*, CityNews, and many other media outlets have interviewed me on this topic.

Accessible – Barrier-Free – Universal Design

Throughout this book, I use the terms "accessible home" and "barrier-free home" interchangeably. I encourage you to decide on your own definition of these terms because what is accessible or barrier-free to you will be unique.

Universal design can more easily be defined. It is a concept that describes environments that are usable by all people regardless of age or ability.

Plan Ahead

Successful chess players strategize and plan at least 3 or 4 moves ahead. Planning ahead is a theme that I stress throughout this book. I think it's the most important advice I can give you. You might not need an accessible, barrier-free home now, but at some point you or someone you care for will.

As you read this book, I encourage you to think like a chess player and start planning ahead!

CHAPTER 1
THE BIG PICTURE

My goal for writing this book is to help you achieve the freedom of a barrier-free home. But first, I think it's important to roll back and first consider the big picture by examining the built environment (human-made structures and landscapes) on a global, national, provincial and local level.

Some individuals who function well in a barrier-free environment can find themselves disabled by design. Our built environment actually creates mobility and other challenges for all kinds of individuals. When the design of the built environment, for instance, fails to account for the diversity of end-users, frustration, segregation and disability are created.

Many of us take the built environment for granted. Where people without mobility issues generally go through their day-to-day tasks with ease, persons with mobility challenges require constant effort and encounter barriers doing the most basic of daily activities, when they are simply trying to enjoy their homes, neighbourhoods and the broader community.

Free movement in public spaces is assumed by most people to be a right. Access to public transportation, ease of movement on streets, entry into and through buildings, and clear routes during emergencies are all elements of an inclusively designed environment. But the design and construction of buildings and places can also create hazards and barriers, thus making the built environment inconvenient, uncomfortable, and unsafe for many when the diversity of the users is not taken into account in the design process.

A space might be rendered inaccessible by the presence or absence of critical physical attributes in the design.

Red Flags:

- Hallways and doorways too narrow for a person using a wheelchair, electric scooter or walker – or for the parent pushing a baby carriage

- Doors too heavy to push open

- Counters too high for a person of short stature or using a wheelchair

- Poor lighting for people with low vision

- Doorknobs too difficult to grasp for people with arthritis

- Parking spaces too narrow for a driver who uses a wheelchair

- Homes and businesses that have stairs to navigate before even getting into the building

- Lack of curb cuts or ramps

- Gravel walkways

- Debris on walkways

- Variations in the grade of walkways

- Hotel rooms that limit access in the bathrooms and even access to the beds

Most disabling architecture stems from 3 issues: changes in level, insufficient space and poor layout or utilization of space.

Howard Gerry, Associate Professor in the Faculty of Design at OCAD University in Toronto, teaches Universal and Accessible Design. He asks the question, "How different would the world be if we designed our homes, buildings, and outdoor spaces with the intent that these environments were to be used and shared by people of all ages and abilities. What if we built environments that were useful for everyone from the ages of 8 to 80 with each individual being able to use the spaces with ease and on an equal basis?"

As Gerry says, "The result would be a more integrated society – one that could be enjoyed by all with dignity and independence. Individuals would have a greater choice in housing along with easier access to employment and services. Not only would individuals be able to stay in their homes longer but they would also be a vital part of the community longer."

The vision is exciting. There is progress being made, although it will not happen overnight.

Global

On a global level, in 2006 the United Nations World Health Organization started the Age-Friendly Cities initiative. The premise is that if cities are designed inclusively for older adults, then everyone – regardless of age or mobility – will be able to actively participate in the community.

National

On a national level, on June 21, 2019, the Accessible Canada Act (Bill C-81) became law. The purpose of this Act is to eliminate and prevent barriers to accessibility in all areas of federal jurisdiction. The Act will establish an organization whose exclusive mandate is to develop accessibility standards.

Provincial

On a provincial level, standards for enhanced access to public spaces are included in the Accessibility for Ontarians with Disabilities Act (AODA.) These standards were phased in between 2015 and 2018 and apply to newly constructed or redeveloped public areas such as recreational trails, outdoor play spaces, sidewalks, walkways and off-street parking.

And as of January 1, 2015, amended requirements and changes to Ontario's Building Code require enhanced accessibility in newly constructed buildings and existing buildings that are scheduled to undergo extensive renovations.

Snapshot of Ontario's Accessibility Rules

- New buildings must provide universal washrooms for men and women, with the lavatory larger than traditional facilities to serve someone in a wheelchair with an assistant.

- Textured strips must be included near ramps, stairs and other elevation changes.

- Doors and corridors must be wider to allow for easier wheelchair access.

- Automatic door openers must be installed.

- Visual fire and smoke alarms must be provided.

- Multi-residential buildings must equip at least 15 percent (up from 10 percent) of suites with accessibility features.

Manitoba and Nova Scotia are following Ontario's lead and creating accessibility laws. These will allow them to develop accessibility standards of their own.

Local

On a local level, Toronto has been recognized as an Age-Friendly City. The City of Toronto's initiative, which started back in 2013, is called "Toronto Senior Strategy 2.0," and I am on the advisory committee. In 2016 the World Health Organization recognized Toronto as an Age-Friendly Community, and its status was renewed in 2018.

For the first time in Toronto's history, there are more people over the age of 65 than children under the age of 15. And the over-65 population is expected to almost double by 2041.

The City of Toronto Council has committed to incorporate age-friendly principles into its new official plan. These recommendations include:

- Creating and funding more senior-friendly (accessible)

public spaces

- Funding home modifications (e.g., accessible entrance solutions and bathroom solutions)
- Improving the accessibility of city streets
- Making the TTC more accessible

In total there are 27 recommendations, and they will help to create a more accessible Toronto.

Toronto is just one example. There are hundreds of Age-Friendly communities across Canada.

Look at the Environment Around You

- What types of environmental or architectural barriers are found in your local environment?
- How prevalent are these barriers?
- To what extent do these barriers limit access for everyone – parents with strollers, persons with disabilities or seniors with mobility challenges?

If accessibility is included in the planning stage rather than approached as an afterthought, the costs would be minimized and the result would typically be more cost-effective.

There is no denying the issues of accessibility are rather complex. There are global, national, provincial and local considerations. Many life situations must be anticipated and provided for through the design of the spaces in which we live. No one knows what tomorrow will bring, but consider how much better our quality of life would be if we could function well in our built environment regardless of any physical limitations we may experience now or in the future.

CHAPTER 2
AGING IN PLACE

"Aging in place" is the notion of planning ahead to ensure you can safely and independently live in your own home for as long as you want. Ideally, your home can be modified to accommodate future mobility challenges, and your surrounding neighbourhood will have the necessary health services, social supports and day-to-day amenities you'll need. Easy access to transportation, pharmacy, grocery store and being near your family and friends are all important considerations.

Older Canadians now represent the fastest-growing segment of our population. By 2030, 23% of the population will be over 65, and the percentage will continue to rise. 85% of Canadians over 55 years old want to age in place in their own home and community for as long as possible. Also worth noting is that home ownership among seniors aged 75+ is on the rise. Seniors are staying in their homes longer and this trend was occurring long before the COVID 19 pandemic. The pandemic will influence even more older adults to age in place in order to provide social separation and the option to safely self-isolate.

Family Caregivers

It's estimated in 2019 that there were 8.5 million family caregivers in Canada, delivering approximately 75% of the care to older adults. Before the pandemic, the number of family caregivers was expected to grow by another 2 million in 2020. Post pandemic, we may see this number increase even further as older adults re-evaluate their housing choices.

Family Caregiver

Aging in place in your own home may not mean the current family home. You may want to consider making a move to a smaller and more accessible home. A reduced lot size, one-floor design and living closer to amenities can all be appealing. It could also mean moving into a home that can accommodate other members of your extended family. I call these multigenerational family homes, and I share an example in Chapter 9.

Your plan may even include making a move from owning to renting. For some, freeing up money from the family home and renting can provide a realistic option where you still live independently but without the worry of home ownership and maintenance.

Simple Modifications Can Often Work

No matter where you choose to live, there are simple modifications that can ensure your safety and independence. The subsequent chapters in this book will discuss many of these simple ideas along with some more involved ideas. It's all about planning ahead!

An assessment with an occupational therapist is a good starting point. Ask for recommendations for how you can live safely and independently in your current home or one you are considering purchasing. A professional contractor who specializes in barrier-free renovations can take those recommendations and determine the physical work required to meet your needs.

Challenges may include:

- Entry to your home
- Narrow doorways
- Stairs to a second floor
- Lack of accessibility in the bathroom, kitchen and laundry room.

To simplify entry to your home, a ramp or platform lift can often be installed at one of the entranceways. Doorways can be widened to ensure the safe passage of a wheelchair or walker. Stairs do not necessarily mean that the upstairs or downstairs is off-limits. Stairlifts, even for stairs with a bend or a landing halfway are available from several companies. An elevator or Telecab are options to consider too.

Bathroom makeovers can be as simple as the installation of grab bars, or more involved modifications that include a walk-in/roll-in shower or a walk-in bathtub. Kitchen modifications might include changes to the counter height or easier access to the sink and appliances. The location of a laundry room can be changed to make washing clothes more manageable. Or hiring some help could mean the laundry room is just fine where it is!

A Little Help Can Go a Long Way

A weekly housekeeper is just one example of a service that could be arranged to keep life simple. Grocery delivery, home care, companion services or help with the outside lawn maintenance or snow removal are all options. And if your aging-in-place plans include a move to a condominium, some of these services will be included in your condo fees.

Whether you plan for modifications in your current home or after making a move to a smaller or multigenerational home, there are numerous services that can help you. These include charities that pick up donations once you begin to declutter, home organizers, haul-away services, and contractors who specialize in barrier-free renovations.

It's common for most people to enlist the help of a financial planner and tax consultant when they plan for retirement. I think it's also prudent to hire a REALTOR® to help you determine the best housing options that are available to meet your needs as you get older.

Is it Practical for You to Age In Place?

Think about your home...

- If you want to live in your current home as you age, what modifications could help you remain independent?

- How will you maintain your home if you need help? Consider what services you might need to hire and the cost. Will you have the money to pay for the services if you need them?

- Do you need to move to a more manageable home? Should you consider a home without stairs?

- What are your housing options if your current home no longer suits your needs?

Think about your community...

- How age-friendly is your community? Determine if you can safely get to stores. Is public transportation accessible?

- What supports and services does your community offer to meet your needs and help you maintain your independence as you age?

- Will you be able to get to the services you need and participate in the activities you enjoy?

- If you are no longer able to drive or choose not to drive, will you have access to reliable and affordable transportation alternatives in your community?

- Are you eligible for any assistance through government or community programs and helping agencies?

- Do you need to consider moving to a community with more services?

Think about additional supports you might need...

- What supports and services are available in your community to help with daily activities such as shopping, cleaning, yard care or snow removal?

- Will you be able to get help with bathing, grooming or other personal supports?

- How much will these services cost? Can you afford them?

- Remember, if you live in a condominium, some of the services such as outdoor maintenance will be covered.

Think about staying connected to your community...

- Is there a local seniors' centre and/or recreation centre nearby?

- Are there organizations you can join or volunteer with? Consider what activities you enjoy doing with others. Will these activities be available to you?

- Where will you find people with similar interests?

- What will you need to do to continue to take part in these activities?

Age is just a number when it comes to dancing!

If you live on your own...

- Will you be able – and interested – in cooking for yourself?

- Will you have access to activities to help you get the exercise you will need to stay healthy?

- How will you be able to stay active – and safe – during all of the seasons, including the winter?

Plan for your financial future...

- What income will you need to maintain your desired

standard of living as you age?

- Do you have a financial plan that includes a plan for addressing emergencies or possible out-of-pocket expenses to support your ability to age in place?

- Are you receiving all the assistance and benefits you may be eligible for?

And finally… if your health begins to fail, do you have someone you can talk with to realistically consider your changing circumstances? At the end of the day, planning and more planning is what will make the difference. When you have realistically thought through your options and all of the 'what if' scenarios, then you are more prepared to make the realistic decisions that may be needed.

CHAPTER 3
ENTRANCE SOLUTIONS

Two key features of a barrier-free entrance include an accessible path of travel and a low- or zero-threshold doorway. These are vital if you use a wheelchair or other mobility devices. And an unobstructed accessible path to your home will minimize or even eliminate the need for assistance.

A home with a barrier-free entrance has many advantages – and not just for those with mobility challenges. It is easier to move items in and out like groceries, recycling and furniture, or to roll a baby stroller inside. It also eliminates the risk of icy stairs in the wintertime.

Ideally, a home should have at least one entrance that provides barrier-free entry. You have lots of options to choose from to improve access into your home. These include landscaped pathways, ramps and mechanical lifts. Additionally, you have the option to locate these changes in the front, side, or rear of the house – and even the garage.

Many homeowners worry that some of the changes will negatively affect the look of their home. But today, barrier-free entranceways are not only functional; they can also be visually appealing.

New home builders have an advantage when designing a home since it's much easier to design and build a home to be barrier-free than it is to retrofit one.

Landscaped Pathways

For existing homes with large front yards, contractors can often develop options through landscaping. Visually, a landscaped pathway that gradually slopes in line with the rising ground can have a beautiful effect. This is accomplished by incorporating a practical design and grading to overcome changes in the elevation of the property. In addition to increasing accessibility, a landscaping solution increases the curb appeal and therefore the resale value of the home.

Landscaped pathway to the front door

Ramps

The most common entrance solution is a wooden ramp. Although much less common, metal ramps are also an option. A variety of ramp configurations can be used, including straight, U-shaped or L-shaped. While ramps are not as visually appealing as a landscaped option, the impact can be softened with landscaping over time. A ramp may be the preferred option for practical or financial reasons.

Wood ramp to the backyard

There are also temporary, portable or modular ramp options that can work in some situations. The use of a ramp does not have to be restricted to provide access to the front of the house. In some cases, the design may be better suited to a side or back entrance.

A professional assessment will be needed to sort out all the variables including the location, slope, length, width, level landings, handrails, and the effects of snow. A ramp that is required to overcome significant changes in level will require a great deal of space. The Ontario Building Code requires ramps to have a minimum of 1-inch (2.54 cm) rise per 12 inches (30.48 cm) of length. However, persons with limited strength may need a more gradual slope. But remember; the more gradual the ramp is, the longer the ramp will have to be. Some properties simply do not have the required space.

Mechanical Lifts

A vertical platform lift, also known as a porch or deck lift, can provide another option. These lifts consist of a platform that is raised and lowered and powered by electricity from a household plug. You can also have a battery backup installed in case the power goes out. The structure is firmly attached to a reinforced concrete pad on the ground. The lift may actually be less expensive than some ramps and takes up much less room.

Platform lift from the deck to the backyard

Garage

When the front, side or back entranceways are not practical, you may be able to create access within your garage. An experienced contractor can determine if there is enough space and ceiling height. One of the advantages of the garage entrance option is the fact that wheels on wheelchairs and mobility devices stay dry in the bad weather. This will help reduce the need to clean the floors inside your house.

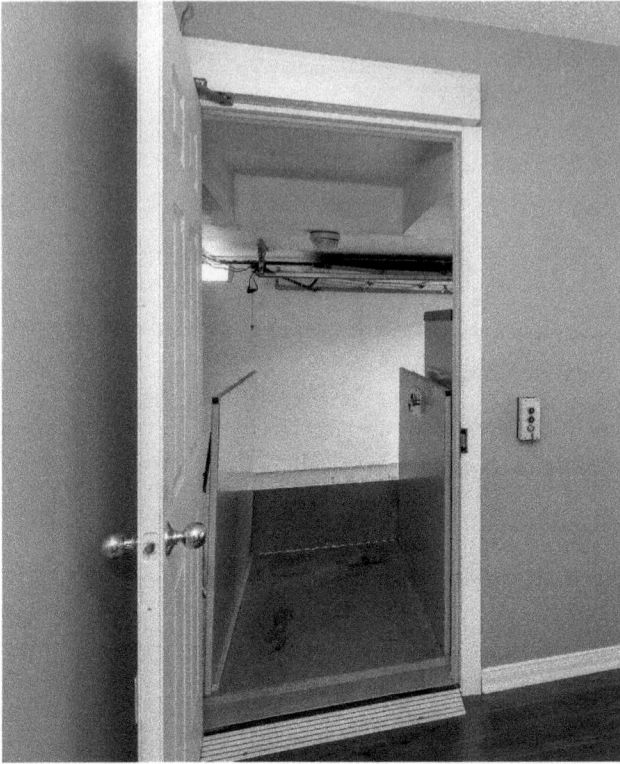

Platform lift from the garage into the home

Getting Through the Door

Traditional doorknobs can be extremely hard for some people to use. The solution could be as simple as installing lever handles which require less dexterity and strength to open. An automatic door and lock opener is also an option. I will discuss these in more detail in the next chapter.

Adding a barrier-free entranceway to your home will increase its accessibility and visitability (I'll talk more about visitability in Chapter 12) while adding to the overall property appeal. As the population ages, any modifications that make access easier will appeal to a broader market.

Plus, a barrier-free entrance says, "Welcome" to everyone!

CHAPTER 4
OPENING DOORS

The expression "Opening Doors" can mean creating opportunities; it can also refer to physically opening a door. This chapter is about both since having a door open automatically for you can create a lot of opportunities at home!

Everyone, regardless of their mobility, has benefited from an automatic door. For example, a parent pushing a stroller or someone carrying groceries will definitely appreciate an automatic door. How many times have you pushed a silver metal circle with the wheelchair symbol on it to open a door? I use them all the time when my hands are full. Sometimes I push them with my knee or my elbow.

Many of my clients rely on door operators as an essential part of their home.

Door operators are most common in commercial buildings, restaurants, retail stores, residential apartment buildings and condominiums. However, more and more door operators are being installed in single-family residential settings. But chances are they were originally designed for commercial/retail use and then modified for residential use.

Circular door activator

Operators for entrance doors and interior doors work on the same principle but require different motors and activators (i.e., buttons and sensors). Assa Abloy, Gyrotech and Stanley are examples of companies that make door operators.

Door operators are powered by electricity. A regular plug outlet connection is adequate. If a wall plug is not available, a new line will need to be installed by an electrician. A typical residential door opener is shown in the picture. The mechanical components, including the motor, are located within the silver rectangular box. A metal arm connects the door to the opener and it moves the door open and closed.

Power door opener

Entrance Door Openers

When it comes to door operators in residential homes, the most common use is on the entrance door – either the accessible entrance door of a house or the front door to a condominium suite.

Entrance doors on houses are often heavy and susceptible to the effects of Mother Nature such as wind and rain. Condominium entrance doors are usually solid fire-rated material and can be subjected to air pressure within the building. Both locations need openers with strong motors.

In addition to powering the door, an entrance opener can be connected to a strike plate mechanism that controls the door latch. This ensures the door can be locked.

Openers can be programmed to keep the door open for a specific period of time. This will vary from person to person depending on their speed of travel.

Interior Door Openers

Interior doors are usually lighter and aren't susceptible to wind or air pressure, so they don't require as much power and therefore can have smaller motors. Interior door latches can be removed so a power strike plate is not necessary.

Activators

To activate a door opener, a sensor needs to be triggered by a door activator. This can be accomplished in a number of ways. The most common is the circular metal button I mentioned earlier. A company called Camden Door Controls has a selection of activator buttons including a 36-inch-long Column™ plate switch. The plate can be pressed from various heights including with a wheelchair foot pedal.

Other options include pressing a button on a remote control, swiping a proximity card (similar to a credit card), a FOB (about the size of a quarter that hangs on a key chain) or movement in front of a motion sensor. For entrance doors that are connected to door locks, a remote control, FOB or proximity card that can be encoded for security is needed.

FOB door activator

Proximity card activator

For condo buildings, proximity cards or FOBs can be programmed to open multiple common-area doors throughout the building including the parking garage entrance. Condo owners usually have a separate door activator for their suite entrance.

Thought needs to be given to the type of door activator that works for you. If you're not able to reach out your arm to swipe a card, then a remote control with a button might be more suitable. If you're looking at buying a condo and need access to the parking garage, this is an important consideration.

Door FOBs can also be used for attendant care staff – to provide access and to track data. I worked with a client who gave all of his attendants their own FOB; they swiped it each time they arrived and left. This information was stored in a computer and helped track staff hours.

As with all home modifications, it's important to do your research to make sure the products you're buying will meet your needs and they are professionally installed.

CHAPTER 5
BATHROOM
SOLUTIONS

A barrier-free entrance solution will get you into your home, and a barrier-free bathroom solution will make it easier for you to stay. A well-designed bathroom can often be the difference between independence and dependence at home.

The majority of household accidents happen in the bathroom, so it makes sense to ensure your bathroom is safe and accommodating to your needs. But bathrooms also present some of the greatest challenges in the home in terms of access and function for people with disabilities, so it's important to take a thoughtful approach to the design.

Roll-In Showers

A roll-in shower is similar to a conventional shower but large enough to accommodate a shower wheelchair or commode and also an attendant if needed. Roll-in shower floors ideally have level thresholds and are slightly slanted to allow the water to drain easily into the floor drain. Depending on your shower design, you may have a circular drain that is centrally located or a trench (rectangular) drain that runs along one side of the shower. A trench drain will only require the floor to be sloped in one direction and therefore may be a safer option.

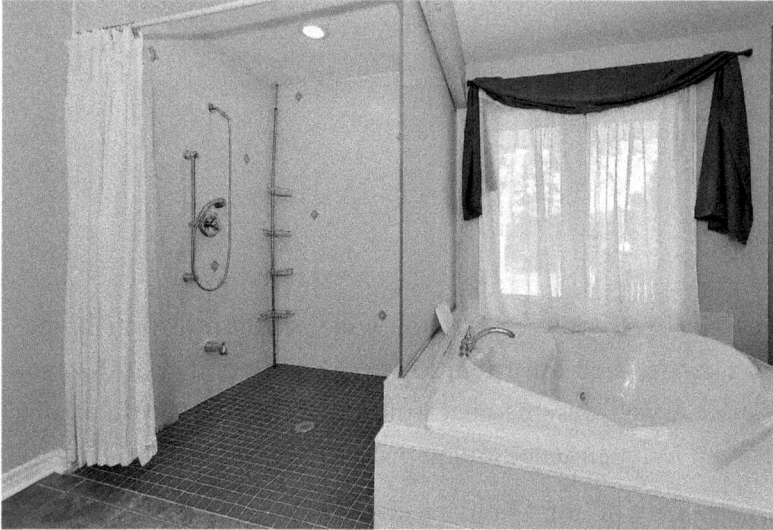

Roll in shower and large tub

If you shower in a seated position, a handheld showerhead with a long hose is a good option. It allows you or an attendant to spray the water where it is needed. With a conventional showerhead, you need to move your body to find the water spray.

A new shower can often go in the same spot as the old tub. This alleviates the need to move the drain and water lines and helps to reduce the costs. This is often a necessity in condominiums since the drains are encased in the concrete floors and cannot be moved. A roll-in shower can be as small as 3 feet (0.91 m) by 3 feet, but 3 feet by 4 feet (1.22 m) or larger is a better choice to allow for easy movement.

Walls throughout the bathroom need to be reinforced to accommodate the placement of grab bars. Floors need to be non-slip. Showerhead controls and niches for shampoo and soap should be accessible from both a seated and standing position. Some roll-in showers are designed without the need for shower curtains or doors.

Benefits are not restricted to the obvious ease of entering, exiting and using the shower. A roll-in shower...

- Is easier to clean

- Can provide additional comfort with an in-shower bench

- Updates the look of your bathroom

- Saves money, since a shower uses about 50% less water than a bathtub

- Is a positive feature for persons of all ages and mobility levels

And any pet owner knows it makes bathing your dog much easier!

Roll in shower with glass door

Roll-Under Sinks

A roll-under sink is also an important part of a barrier-free bathroom. Sinks can be mounted directly to the wall, or incorporated into a vanity. It's important to determine the ideal height for you to efficiently and safely use the sink. Ensure that you've got clearance above your knees if you'll be rolling under the sink. For brushing your teeth, you'll need to lean over the sink basin. Are there foot pedals that extend in front of your chair? How much space do you need on the vanity for your bathroom kit? And a bathroom mirror that can tilt up and down will ensure everyone who uses the bathroom can get the perfect view.

Roll under sink

How close do you need to be to the taps and faucet? They are usually mounted on the far side of the sink; however, some sink designs can accommodate them to be mounted on the side of the sink which requires less reaching. And if turning the taps on or off is a challenge, install an automatic faucet. Just set the desired temperature and each time you place your hands under the sensor, the water will flow.

Toilets

Toilet location is vital to a well-designed bathroom. Similar to determining the ideal configuration of a roll-under sink, your toilet location and height needs to be planned out to meet your unique needs. Toilet technology has come a long way in recent years so do your research to find the ideal make and model.

If you transfer from a wheelchair onto the toilet, you'll want to have open space on your preferred transfer side. If you use a commode chair, removing the toilet seat will allow for better positioning over the top of the toilet.

Toilets come in a wide range of heights. Standard toilet height is considered to be approximately 14 -15 inches high measured from the floor to the rim, not including the toilet seat. Right-height or comfort-height models are 15 -17 inches high and tall-height toilets are 17 - 20 inches. Home Depot also carries a model that is 10.3 inches in height.

A product called the Toilevator will raise the height of your existing toilet by 3.5 inches. It works like a pedestal and is secured to the floor above your existing waste pipe, and your toilet is secured on top. This product eliminates the need for a raised toilet seat which is often unsafe, unsightly and unsanitary. The Toilevator can be easily found via an online search.

Toilevator

Another product that is still in the concept phase is called the ToiLocator (This is different than the app of the same name that finds the closest public toilet). The ToiLocator allows the toilet to be repositioned in a bathroom to make it more accessible, as well as raising the height of the toilet. An added waste pipe extends from the toilet towards the original waste pipe so that a reconstruction of the bathroom layout is not necessary. This product concept has great potential to facilitate a quick, cost-effective toilet solution.

ToiLocator

You'll want to make sure the toilet paper dispenser and a spare roll are within reach. Alternatively, bidet attachments can be added to most toilets and be connected to the same water supply line. All models have a hands-free cleaning spray, while more elaborate models also offer drying, adjustable water temperature, heated seat and night-light options.

Grab Bars

Carefully plan out the configuration and location of grab bars and drop-down bars for safe transferring. Your reinforced bathroom walls will ensure they can be attached securely. There is a large selection of grab bars available, including decorative ones so you can choose the style, colour, and finish that suits you and your décor best.

Bathtubs

You may prefer soaking in a bathtub, rather than showering. There have been some great advances to make bathtubs more accessible in addition to supplying many spa-like features. Safety is paramount, so ensure you have a non-slip surface, reinforced grab bars and a flat-bottomed tub to provide stability. There are a variety of mechanical lifts that can assist getting you in and out of the tub. Ceiling track lifts, floor lifts and seats that lower down into the tub are all options. And there are many bath bench options that fit within the bathtub, and ones that extend over the side of the tub if you want to shower in a seated position.

A walk-in tub is another option to consider. This type of tub is ideal for persons with limited balance and agility. They have a door that opens outward and a bench seat so you can step into the tub, sit down and close the door. When the door is shut it creates a watertight seal. The tub fills up (and drains when you're done) while you're sitting in it and there is a handheld spray for showering your upper body. Consider installing a heat light above the tub or a buying a model that has a quick drain option so you don't get cold waiting for the water to drain at the end of your bath.

Walk in tub

If you've got enough space, consider installing a tub and shower. This will allow for more flexibility in the future if your needs change. And if you add features such as heated flooring, multiple showerheads and towel heaters – your bathroom will look and feel more like a high-end spa!

CHAPTER 6
LET'S GET COOKING

The kitchen has become the epicentre of the home – often replacing the living room and family room as the spot family and friends congregate. Not surprising, people want functional, usable and flexible kitchen designs that work for everyone in the family. And an accessible kitchen is no different. It has to incorporate the unique needs of the family while preserving the warm atmosphere designed to welcome guests.

Kitchen with lowered roll under counters and island

A flexible kitchen design must ensure the sink, worktop, equipment, appliances and storage can all be easily accessed and are easy to use from both a standing and seated position. Traditionally, kitchen designers focused on a compact work triangle including the sink, stove and refrigerator. But today, with more attention to everyone's needs, the triangle has to be expanded to include all work areas as well as a separate cooktop and wall oven, dishwasher and disposal of compost, recycling and garbage.

Good design is the foundation of an efficient and accessible kitchen that maximizes independence and convenience.

Kitchen with lowered roll under counters

Canada Mortgage and Housing Corporation has identified some important considerations in accessible kitchen design:

- The kitchen layout must provide the right balance between the countertop area, manoeuvring space and storage space.

- Kitchen size for someone who uses a walker or wheelchair should allow manoeuvring space of 30 inches by 47 inches (750 mm x 1200 mm) in front of controls, work areas and appliances. This work area can be part of the overall required minimum manoeuvring space of 59 inches by 59 inches (1500 mm x 1500 mm) in the work triangle. Power wheelchair and scooter users will need a larger turning radius.

- Minimal-effort design takes into account the location and relationship of all major elements within the kitchen and can include more lighting, a place to sit while working, a lower work station and accessible storage.

- Adaptability addresses the needs of persons in wheelchairs as well as those who are ambulant. Finding an effective height for the countertop, sink, cooktop, worktop and upper cabinets can be challenging. There are both high-tech and low-tech design options.

- Ease of cleaning versus trends such as stainless steel has to be taken into account. Appliances, floors and countertop surfaces must be low maintenance.

The major design elements of a barrier-free kitchen are countertops; cupboards, drawers and pantries; sinks and cleanup areas; food preparation areas; switches and controls; interior finishing; lighting; and audibility of such things as timers and smoke alarms.

Randy Sora, Accessibility Design/Management Consultant at EZaccess Inc. describes his approach to designing accessible kitchen layouts to meet his client's specific needs:

"I generally develop the design myself in consultation with the client and occupational therapist. Once we get to the general configuration and placement of appliances, storage, work areas, etc., I then hand it over to the kitchen designer to fine-tune. They provide their input into customizing, identify hurdles that we may face or suggest additional ideas. It's definitely a collaborative process."

Deborah Damiano, the Sales Manager at Paddy's Market, "The Appliance Specialist," supplies accessible kitchen appliances:

"We work with each customer to identify their unique needs. For instance, refrigerators that are counter depth can be easier to access. The fridge on top and freezer on the bottom can also be helpful, as well as swing doors or even fridge drawers that pull out. Wall ovens with swing doors are also easier to use than an oven with a drop-down door. Technology has also improved cooktops; the induction cooktop is extremely safe, automatically shutting off if the pot has been removed. The burners also cool off as soon as the pot is taken off the burner. The options are increasing, giving customers much more choice than in the past."

Kitchen with roll under counters and lowered upper cabinets

Huge advances have been made in both kitchen design and technology, helping to ensure everyone can enjoy the kitchen equally and safely. However, changes should not be made in isolation. Professional advice, flexible solutions and long-range planning can make all the difference in the world.

CHAPTER 7
REACHING THE UPPER KITCHEN SHELVES

Reaching the upper-cupboard shelves in the kitchen can be a challenge for everyone but is especially true if you use a wheelchair.

I recently sold a preconstruction condo that included a wheelchair-accessible kitchen. The buyer is a paraplegic and likes to cook. And while he is excited to have a kitchen with lowered counters, roll-under sink and cooktop, side-opening wall oven, and drawer dishwasher, he also wants use of the upper kitchen cupboards.

This inspired me to do some research on lowering the upper kitchen-cupboard shelves. In my search, I found both manual pull-down options and fully automated options.

Manual Pull-Down Options

There are several manual pull-down shelf options available in the marketplace and all of them require some arm strength. You'll need to open the cupboard door and reach up and pull out and then down on the inner shelf handle. The shelves are attached to the sides of the inner cupboard by mechanical arms that have springs or gears which allow the shelves to extend out and lower down.

A company called Richelieu sells pull-down shelves from a variety of manufacturers. They have a showroom near the Toronto airport where I was able to try out four different brands of pull-down shelves.

The only pull-down option that I'm going to highlight is the Rev-A-Shelf 5PD Series. This shelf can be installed at the lowest point of the upper cabinet and it has a rubber-handle grip attached to two shelves that pull out 14 ¾ inches and down 10 inches towards you. When the shelf is lowered, it locks into place. To unlock it, you just need to tug on the handle and the shelf raises itself back into the cupboard without any further effort required.

Pull down shelf upper position   Pull down shelf lower position

Automated Options

I've seen two kinds of automated upper-cupboard shelves. The first kind is where the whole cupboard (doors and shelves) lowers down. The second is where just the shelving unit lowers down.

Lowering the Whole Cupboard

When the whole cupboard is lowered, it is brought down to the counter height by a mechanical frame that is attached to the back of the cupboard and powered by a small electrical motor. The overall cupboard depth is reduced to accommodate this frame. The countertop needs to be clear of any items so the cupboard can sit flush on the counter.

Lowering cupboard upper position

Lowering cupboard lower position

For ease of removing or replacing items in the cupboard, you'll want to have additional counter space nearby that can be reached when the cupboard is in the lowered position and the doors are open.

Lowering the Shelf

Similar to the manual pull-down shelf option, lowering just the shelf keeps the cupboard doors in place and brings only the interior shelf to a lower level.

Simple Freedom Design Ltd. is a Canadian company located in Southwestern Ontario, and they can create a custom solution to automate your existing cabinets. They retain your existing cabinet doors and appearance but they will remove the internal shelving and replace it with a fully automated system. The upper shelf will be reduced in size to make room for the motor. This system will allow you to remotely lower and raise the shelves. Yves Trottier, one of the principal partners, says each installation is customized for their specific client.

Lowering shelf

A company in Sweden called Granberg Interior manufactures a line of automated kitchen cupboards and shelves. They don't have a distributor in North America but their products can be purchased through Versatile Accessibility, a home modification company located in Markham Ontario.

All of the automated options require access to an electrical plug.

For aesthetics, having the plug located on top of the cupboards will allow the wires to remain hidden. I encourage new home builders and homeowners who are renovating to plan ahead and install extra outlets above all upper cupboards. This will make it much easier for future automation.

Whether you choose the manual pull-down shelf option or the automated option, it'll be much easier to reach items in your upper kitchen cupboards.

CHAPTER 8
HOME OFFICE

The COVID 19 pandemic has made the home office a vital part of almost everyone's home. Working from home was gaining popularity leading up to 2020, and it will now become the accepted and expected norm for many jobs going forward.

Working from home

Innovations in technology and furniture design have made it easier for everyone, including people with disabilities, to work from home.

The Rick Hansen Foundation, in one of their recent initiatives, turned an inaccessible office into one that accommodates people who use wheelchairs. In their design, they opted for an open-concept layout that allowed wheelchair users to have space to turn around, lots of natural light and electric adjustable-height desks.

I reached out to Jim Lorefice, the Founder of Top Lawyers. The company is headquartered on Bloor Street in Toronto, but Jim handles his responsibilities from his home office. I asked Jim to describe his accessible home office and what advice he has for someone setting up their own office.

"A home office has so many advantages. Not having to commute is a huge time saver and gain in productivity. Not having to worry about parking or accessibility issues is another plus. In terms of my home office setup and advice, I would offer… Ikea and technology are your best friends.

"My home office furniture is all Ikea. Their clever designs lend themselves to ease of use by anybody regardless of ability. I love my height-adjustable desk. In terms of technology, it's such an equalizer. My advice to others would be to not skimp on the tech that boosts your productivity and puts you on a level playing field with your able-bodied peers. My PC is a beast. It allows me to run the demanding programs I use, including a web server for offline website builds. Two items I couldn't be without are my Bluetooth headset and Blue microphone. The headset allows me to communicate clearly when handling calls, and the mic is amazing for online collaboration and speech to text.

"Whatever your setup, make sure you are comfortable. You're going to need to put in the time to find success."

Research has shown that in the last 15 years, there has been an increase in initiatives to help those with severe disabilities enter the job market. And having the option of working from home can provide great benefits:

- Less stress related to getting to and from work

- Flexible schedule

- Personal needs can be more easily taken care of

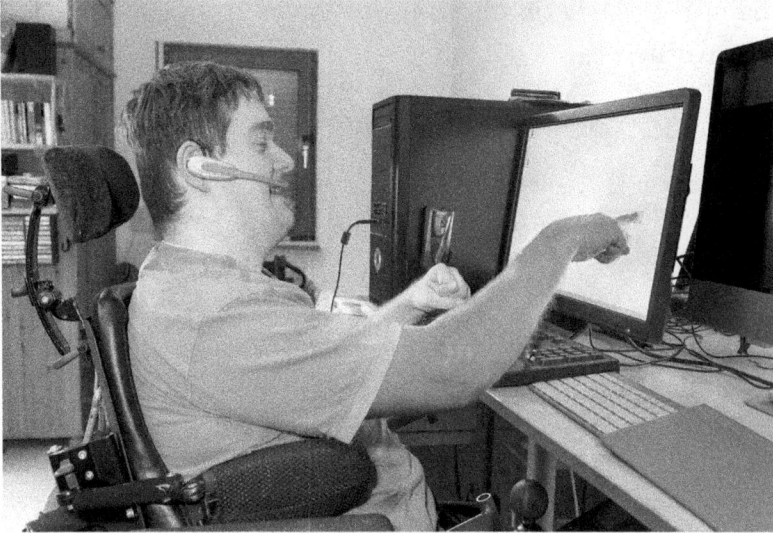

Home office

The first stage in designing a home office space is deciding what you need. One person's office layout may not be suitable for everyone, so take the time to plan. Good design will lead to an efficient and accessible space.

Adaptive Computing

Adaptive computing refers to a computer system, both hardware and software, that can be customized for people with disabilities. An example of adaptive computing is the JAWS® (Job Access With Speech) program which was developed for computer users with vision loss. JAWS® acts as a screen reader that reads the text on your screen. It allows the user to surf the internet, write a document and read and respond to emails. It can also be connected via Bluetooth to a braille embosser. This device has the ability to change the raised dots on a device based on what is happening on the screen so the user can follow along and navigate.

Keyboard with braille

Other examples of adaptive computing can include sip-and-puff systems that are activated by inhaling or exhaling; joysticks that can be controlled by hand, feet or chin; and wands that can press keys on a keyboard and can be worn on the head, held in the mouth or strapped to the chin.

Lighting

The lighting in your home office is very important. Natural light helps job performance and enhances overall well-being according to a survey done by Harvard Business Review. Opting for a bigger window instead of an overhead light is proven to make working at home more comfortable. If a big window isn't possible, try incorporating a variety of lighting options. Desk lamps for reading and closet lighting should be considered too. To activate the lights, try using easy-to-reach switches that are motion detected or activated by voice.

Storage

Storage in your office is important as well. You want to be able to reach all areas within the storage space. Whether that means taking the doors off a closet or having low shelves, it is worth planning.

Furniture

After figuring out your personal and work needs, the final stage is choosing the furniture and planning the layout of the room. Make sure you have a desk that is the right height and there is adequate space to manoeuvre within your space. If you have vision loss, try placing different textures to guide you to places like your chair and computer. These can include a strip of carpet along the wall leading to your desk or raised bumps to indicate where certain items are stored.

The goal is independence and productivity from your home office – but that doesn't mean it has to be boring. Find furniture and decorations that fit your style and make you want to spend time there. Taking the extra time to design a space that is accessible and enjoyable will be worth it.

CHAPTER 9
NEED A LIFT?

If you need wheelchair access within your home, a home elevator can be a viable solution. Residential elevators were not feasible for many homes in the past; however, newer technology has made it easier to retrofit them into existing homes. And more and more new-construction homes are including them.

The definition of "elevator" is changing. Traditionally, all elevators were fully enclosed in a hoistway or shaft, but this is no longer the case. Integrated hoistways and Telecabs now provide a lot of flexibility for elevator designs.

Traditional Elevators

Traditional residential elevators that are built in an enclosed hoistway can raise and lower weights up to 1500 lbs (680 kg) between multiple floors. These types of elevators can be customized: automatic doors, lighting, operating controls, handles, interior and exterior finishes are just some of the items you can style to your own specifications.

Traditional residential elevator

I sold a home that had been retrofitted into a multigenerational home with an elevator. The owner had converted the house into three separate flats, removed the central staircase and connected all three levels with an elevator. The owner lived on the second floor, her mother lived on the main floor and the two daughters lived on the lower level. Each had a self-contained apartment with a separate entrance. Each member of the family maintained their independence and privacy while still being able to freely visit each other for meals or to offer assistance when needed.

Integrated Hoistway Elevators

Integrated hoistway elevators have a self-supporting frame that is built into the design. This frame gives you a lot of flexibility for placement within your home. And it allows the elevator to have large windows that let in a lot of light and help to reduce the feeling of being in a confined space. More and more companies are offering innovative elevator designs that utilize an integrated hoistway. Load capacity can go up to approximately 950 lbs (430 kg) and higher depending on the design and mechanics.

Integrated hoistway elevator

Vacuum Elevators

The Pneumatic Vacuum Elevator (PVE) utilizes an integrated hoistway, but it uses atmospheric pressure to raise and lower. Pneumatic tubes go back to the late 19th century where they were used in banks and department stores to send small packages and notes quickly from one area to another.

You might remember an imagined version of the PVE in the futuristic cartoon show from the 1960s called *The Jetsons*.

A PVE can be incorporated into new home construction and home modification projects. They are revolutionary for a number of reasons. Installation is much simpler; they can be fitted almost anywhere in your home. No excavation or large mechanical room is needed – the elevator simply rests on the existing floor. They do not require cables, chains, pistons or counterweights. The elevator is composed of two perfectly fitted parts that support precise atmospheric pressure above and below the cab. Basically, the lifting action occurs when pressure is reduced above the cab, causing it to rise to fill the void. To descend, a control valve slowly releases pressure, creating a cushion of air beneath the cab. The largest models of PVE have a load capacity of approximately 525 lbs (238 kg).

Pneumatic vacuum elevator

I've had the pleasure of working with two families who have vacuum elevators in their homes. The first one was capable of carrying a person in a power chair and a second person standing. The other was much smaller, designed to carry one person standing. Both elevators were part of a modification to the original space.

Telecab

A Telecab is an enclosed elevator that can be used between two floors, ideal where space is at a premium. It can be installed more easily than a traditional elevator because it requires minimum preparation as it has no walls or shaft. It is sometimes referred to as a shaftless elevator. The Telecab operates on a track that is mounted to a load-bearing wall. When not in use, the elevator can be sent to the other floor, allowing for use of the entire room. The largest model Telecab has a weight capacity of approximately 845 lbs (383 kg).

My parents installed a Telecab in their home. It took many years of encouraging them to plan ahead so they could continue to live independently in the home they love before they finally installed one. Looking back now, they both agree it was a great decision.

With so many elevator choices to consider, you'll need to research to find out what makes and models are best suited to your needs. Regardless of the type of elevator you choose, you'll want to have regular maintenance and safety inspections done to ensure it continues to run smoothly and safely. Install a phone inside the unit in case you need assistance and for even more peace of mind, some elevator companies offer remote monitoring for service interruptions.

Jeffrey Kerr and a Telecab elevator

Elevators increase accessibility for the whole family. Costs will vary depending on the type you choose. And although an elevator will be more expensive than other mechanical options like a stair glide, it is often more practical in the long term because it's suitable for everyone regardless of their age or mobility.

CHAPTER 10
ENABLED GARDENS

Enabled gardens can be a great outdoor addition to an accessible home. Gardening is a constant exercise of the imagination, but it's so much more. Doctors have long praised the benefits and health advantages of gardening which include:

- Being outside – exposure to vitamin D
- Decrease in dementia risk
- Mood-boosting benefits
- Helps with combatting loneliness
- Better sleep
- Stress reduction

My wife is an avid gardener. She has created a vegetable garden in one corner of our backyard, a flower bed in the other. Her favourites are the containers dotted around the house, from fragrant herbs and tomatoes to strawberries and flowers that bloom from spring to fall.

Gardening is Therapeutic

Gardening has long been considered therapeutic. Spending time in a natural landscape can assist in relaxation, meditation, as well as providing peace and beauty. Those who love to garden are passionate and already have a strong connection to nature and shouldn't lose this.

Horticultural therapy, which uses nature as therapy, dates back to 1812 and has been shown to help people who are physically disabled as well as those with mental health challenges. It can be an important part of recovery and care.

With all the physical and mental benefits, it is possible to find happiness in the dirt. But what can you do when your body faces challenges that prevent the kneeling, stooping and squatting that's necessary for traditional gardening?

Enabled or Raised Gardens

An enabled or raised garden allows people with limited mobility to grow vegetables, herbs and flowers. The garden can be raised to a height that's comfortable for you.

A quick internet search for raised beds gives suggestions for the best types of wood if you want to construct it from scratch. For some, it may be just as easy to buy a kit. I've found kits that range from very affordable, to some that are high-end and positively decadent looking. There are some available for every budget at your local Home Depot, or online at Amazon, Lee Valley or even Wayfair.

Custom made enabled or raised garden

What to Use in Your Garden

Rocks and stones can be used at the bottom to allow for drainage as excess moisture can damage the roots of delicate plants. I've discovered a "lasagna method" works well over top of the rocks – a mixture of leaves, grass clippings and other organic material such as wood chips with a layer of cardboard. This will break down into nice compost over time.

On top of this, add a mixture of topsoil, compost, and organic material such as manure to give plants a nutrient-rich soil.

As for planting – whatever you like! What's your favourite vegetable?

The challenge will be to allow enough space since overcrowded plants tend not to fair well with the competition for water, nutrients and sunlight, not to mention root space. The location of certain plants is important; for example, try not to have the more delicate lettuces beside the sprawling cucumber. Stakes, ladders, and cages can help make the garden more manageable as well as give a neater appearance.

Also, beds can be planted with durable plants with different textures and smells for blind gardeners.

Enabled or raised garden box

If you're maintaining multiple beds, create a wide, level pathway between them to allow access for your wheelchair or mobility device. And remember to make the centre of the bed accessible for watering and weeding.

Not only do raised gardens eliminate many of the physical tasks that come with caring for large garden plots – making them beneficial for those with disabilities – they are a plus for every gardener. They allow you to plant earlier because the container soil warms more easily and earlier in the year, the soil is better since you're starting from the best and there will be fewer weeds.

Along with raised beds, there are a wide range of extendable and adaptive tools available for your use. Or your tools can be a DIY project; foam tubes can be placed over handles to give added length or better grip, or arm splints can be added for extra support. Even pipe insulation and hockey tape can quickly help with the grip on trowels and pruning shears.

can be painted with bright colours to stand out among the browns and greens of the garden, and ribbons or cords can be attached to handles to prevent dropping or misplacing tools.

to the growing trend of raised or enabled gardens, gardening can be done standing or sitting. You can continue to enjoy your gardening hobby regardless of your challenges.

CHAPTER 11
TECHNOLOGY, ASSISTIVE DEVICES AND RESEARCH

Innovations in home automation, smart home technology, home care technology and assistive devices will help you live safely and independently in your home and community.

Home automation, like the kitchen cupboards described in Chapter 6 and the automatic door operators in Chapter 4, can perform important tasks for people with physical or cognitive disabilities.

People with disabilities are often very quick to adopt innovations that improve their independence. In many cases, caregivers will be the first adopters of innovations to help them care for aging family members.

Consider the remote control. It was originally developed to help people with limited mobility control their environment, not just their TVs. Now, remote controls are used by everyone. It would be hard to imagine a television set without one. The electric toothbrush is another example. It was developed to help people with limited mobility brush their teeth, and now they've become a common household item.

Smart Home Technology

For many, smart home technology is absolutely essential for their independence. Living in their own home would not be possible without it.

Novalte has designed smart home technology called emitto to help older adults and people with disabilities live independently. I have a client who uses emitto and he has it integrated with Google Home to control many of the features in his home environment. He can control his front door, room lighting, window blinds, TV and adjustable bed using voice commands through his smartphone. Visit the company website for a video demonstration: www.Novalte.ca

Smart ONE Solutions is a company that is developing technology for smart homes, buildings, communities and cities. Their vision is to connect individual smart units in a condominium community with a common management platform and user experience. The long-range plan is to connect the smart communities together within a city. A virtual lobby entry system, parcel notification, parking, security, resident services and building common areas can all be connected. On a bigger scale, a virtual mall with grocery, shops and services can also be integrated. Learn more at: www.Smartone.solutions

Home automation and smart home technology have a number of benefits, including:

• Increasing an individual's independence by providing greater control of the home environment

• Making it easier to communicate with family and friends and reducing isolation

- Improving personal safety
- Reducing heating and cooling costs
- Increasing the home's energy efficiency
- Providing both audible and visual alerts to emergency situations
- Allowing home monitoring while away

Sensors

There are a variety of products that rely on sensors. For instance, blood pressure, pulse rate, breathing patterns, and glucose can be regularly monitored by wearing a band around your wrist. The information can be transmitted directly by the device to a healthcare professional – or can be viewed by a visiting a health care provider. These bands can also help track sleep, diet and steps taken – all valuable information for monitoring health.

Sensors can also be placed around the home, for instance on doors and windows, as well as in appliances. They alert caregivers via a smartphone app if the individual misses a meal, doesn't get out of bed, falls or is inactive too long. Alerts can also be set up for someone leaving the house or leaving the water running past the designated time. This type of technology can be very helpful for monitoring individuals with Alzheimer's, helping them to remain at home longer.

GPS

When people are away from home, GPS tracking technology allows families, health workers, or law enforcement professionals to locate them in case of emergency. The technology also senses if users fall, and automatically calls for assistance even if the wearer is incapacitated.

Smartphones, Mobile Apps and the Internet

Mobile apps for smartphones offer both monitoring and communication. For instance, individuals can get in touch with their caregiver with a few taps on their phone, and reminder apps can notify them about medications or appointments.

The use of smartphones and the internet has evolved to the point where you can get immediate health care information and advice any time of the day including:

- Live professionals (e.g., registered nurses, pharmacists)
- Reminders (e.g., medications, appointments)
- Technical 'how to' help with medical/health devices
- Personal health records
- Coaching services to encourage healthy lifestyle changes

The KITE Research Institute

Innovation is one of the four founding pillars at the University Health Network's KITE Rehabilitation Institute, located in Toronto. It is the number one rehabilitation research institute in the world. KITE stands for Knowledge, Innovation, Talent, Everywhere.

KITE research lab

KITE is a state-of-the-art research facility. It provides a unique network of cutting-edge labs where researchers develop technology and test ideas in a realistic setting. Their results are evident in new therapies and products and prototypes for academic and business partners.

KITE is focused on:

- Preventing illness and injury by making streets, homes and workplaces safer – and keeping people out of the hospital.

- Devising new and more effective rehabilitation treatments, assistive devices and technologies to maximize recovery for people with disabilities, illness and age-related conditions – so they can live life to the fullest.

- Helping people live longer and more safely in their own homes as they age, with the support of advanced technologies and products.

The "Home Lab" at KITE is a testament to the investment being made to translate research findings into practical outcomes, helping people better manage disabilities including disabilities that come from growing older.

Some of the products appear so simple, yet they bring adaptive devices to a new level for the consumer. Two products that were developed at KITE that are already making life easier for many, are the Toilevator® and the EasyRange™ Pole System. The Toilevator® was highlighted in Chapter 5.

The EasyRange™ Pole System is a modular system for safer in-home mobility. It addresses the need to provide safer walking and transferring without having to modify your home by drilling into the walls and floors. It is a modular system of pressure-fitted vertical grab poles and clip-on horizontal rails. It can be easily installed and moved when it's no longer needed. As a result of the flexible design, the poles can also serve as parallel bars, an extra handrail support on stairs, and any other personalized arrangements you need. You can find out more online at **www.HartMobility.com**

EasyRange™ pole system

KITE is also involved in a variety of projects to address fall prevention. Falls remain a leading cause of injury, disability, and death. Well-designed handrails are the most effective safety and accessibility features that we can add to stairs, ramps and other walkways to prevent falls, promote balance, and encourage safe walking. However, handrails are often too high or too low or do not have a shape that is easy or comfortable to grasp.

The KITE team is using a variety of approaches to help them understand the forces exerted by muscles and gravity on the body to determine what comprises 'optimal' and 'acceptable' handrail heights and style to promote balance recovery and prevent falls. This will provide evidence-based recommendations for handrail design that can inform building codes, accessibility standards, and guidelines for consumers who are installing handrails in their homes.

The research at KITE results in practical real-life solutions to many challenges faced by persons with disabilities or illness and age-related conditions. Their products support both the individual and the caregiver.

CHAPTER 12
VISITABLE HOMES

Whose house for the holidays? This is a question I like to ask to illustrate the importance of a visitable home.

For many people, family gatherings happen at a location that is accessible to the whole family. This was certainly the case for many years at my family get-togethers as we always included my Aunt Jeane in our celebrations. Because of MS, she used a wheelchair for mobility which meant gathering at a home that had an accessible entrance and main-floor bathroom.

Visitable housing or visitability is the concept of designing and building homes with basic accessibility in place. Visitable homes provide easy access to the main level for everyone, even if no one in the home currently requires barrier-free features. Visitable housing serves two purposes: it offers convenience for the home's residents and a welcoming environment for visitors of all ages and mobility levels.

Visitable homes have three basic features:

- An entranceway at the front, side or back of the home that is free of steps

- Wider doorways – at least 34 inches (850 mm) – and a clear passage from room to room on the main floor

- A powder room or main bathroom that can be accessed by visitors who use mobility devices

Accessible main floor two piece washroom

History

Visitable housing was first introduced in North America in 1986. Eleanor Smith and a group of advocates for people with physical disabilities were involved in a Habitat for Humanity housing development in Atlanta. Some of the new homes incorporated best practices for accessibility, but residents soon learned that although their own homes were perfect for their needs, they could not visit their neighbours who had stairs at the entranceways and inaccessible bathrooms. Change began at the grassroots level and is now an international movement.

The trend toward visitable housing has been gaining attention throughout the US, Australia, the United Kingdom, some European countries and now Canada. VisitAble Housing Canada, an initiative of the Canadian Centre on Disability Studies, is advocating for change with policymakers and new home builders.

Traditionally, homes were built to accommodate the immediate needs of young buyers in their 20s, 30s and 40s. They were not designed for these same people to age in place. Fortunately, today more and more architects and home builders are becoming aware of barrier-free and universal design. It's not practical to include a long list of accessibility features in every new home, but in most locations, it is practical to include the 3 key features mentioned above when the house is being built. It is always more affordable to build in the features you want at the beginning. The cost increases when you have to make changes after the fact or when you retrofit an older home.

Finding Solutions

A visitable home needs a step-free entrance. When houses are close together and lot sizes are small, there usually isn't enough space to build a ramp, and a mechanical lift is often the only option for an accessible entrance. Landscaping can be utilized when there is enough outdoor space around your home.

Once inside, a visitable home needs a main-floor bathroom. However, finding a home with one can be a challenge. And if there is a main floor bathroom, they are often very small and tucked away – and rarely large enough for a person using a wheelchair to access. This is when some creative solutions may be necessary like relocating the bathroom vanity. I'm seeing more and more restaurants with open-concept wash stations outside the toilet stalls. Why not consider that option at home?

Door hinges that swing out, or pocket doors, allow more space within the bathroom. And temporary screens and curtains can also be used.

Guest bathroom at my client's home

CMHC

The Canadian Mortgage and Housing Corporation (CMHC) has published a number of fact sheets on visitable homes. Here are four benefits highlighted by CMHC:

Convenience: There's easy access for aging parents, young children, parents with strollers, and visitors who use a wheelchair – as well as for moving heavy items.

Community: It creates an accommodating environment for residents of all ages, especially for the elderly, where everyone feels welcome and engaged.

Comfort: A spacious open-concept home with large doorways and hallways makes moving around easier and provides pleasing esthetics; plus there's less risk of falls and injury caused by steps.

Maintenance: No front steps makes snow shovelling a little easier in the winter.

A home that is built or renovated with visitability in mind becomes more valuable in the long term. As the homeowners themselves age, the changes for visitability also support aging in place. Anyone with a mobility challenge will be less likely to have to move when their home is equipped with some accessibility features.

CHAPTER 13
THE OCCUPATIONAL THERAPIST

When you decide to buy an accessible home, in addition to working with a REALTOR®, I recommend consulting with an occupational therapist (OT).

According to the Canadian Association of Occupational Therapists:

"Occupational therapy is a type of health care that helps to solve the problems that interfere with a person's ability to do the things that are important to them.

Everyday things like:

- Self-care – getting dressed, eating, moving around the house
- Being productive – going to work or school, participating in the community
- Leisure activities – sports, gardening, social activities"

Are You Working with an OT?

One of the questions I always ask my clients is, "Are you working with an occupational therapist?" I recommend talking with an OT to ask for recommendations regarding activities of daily living. What are your needs now? How about in 5 years? In 10 years? Your future mobility needs require careful consideration to ensure you make the right move.

Throughout my 21+ year career in real estate, I have received many phone calls from people who were forced to make a second move because their long-term needs were not well thought out the first time.

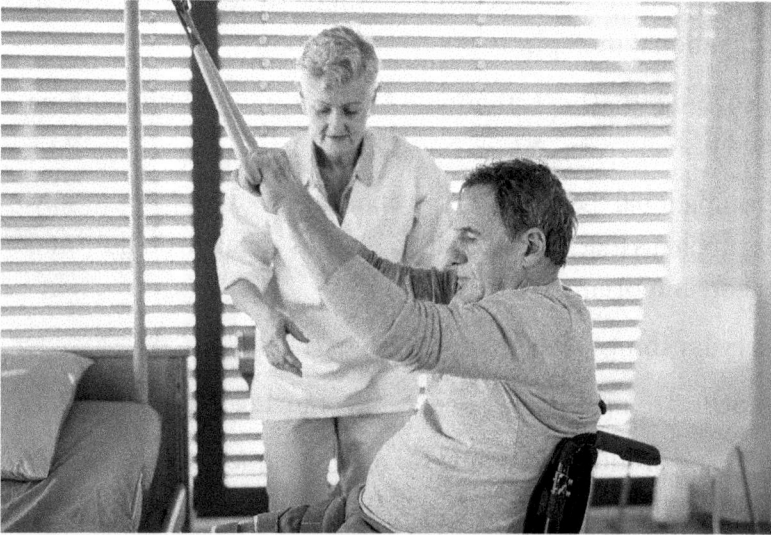

Working with an OT

It's far better to buy a home that can be modified to accommodate your future needs. Will you need an accessible entrance? How about an accessible bathroom? Will you need access to a second floor or basement? An OT can help you with all of these answers.

And with the right home, these features can always be added at a later date.

OTs can be a valuable resource to help you age in place. An OT can make recommendations for present-day needs and potential future needs. If your current home can be modified to meet your future needs, then great! However, if it can't be modified cost-effectively or you'd simply prefer to move, now is the time to start planning. When it comes to housing, always plan ahead; be proactive rather than reactive.

OTs are also a very important part of the rehab team after an injury or accident. I regularly get asked to consult on housing after a motor vehicle accident or other personal injury (see the next chapter on Post-Accident Housing Options.) The request often comes from the OT who is already working with the client. If it's determined that the pre-accident home can't be modified, and the client decides to move, I rely on the OT to provide me with a list of essentials the new home needs to have.

Whether you're making a move to an accessible home, modifying your existing home or planning to age in place, an occupational therapist will have valuable insight and advice.

CHAPTER 14
POST-ACCIDENT HOUSING OPTIONS

Sometimes it's not always possible to plan ahead for your housing needs. If you've been in a traumatic accident (like a motor vehicle crash) and sustained physical injury, you may suddenly need to make a move if your pre-accident home can no longer meet your needs.

I have worked with many clients who have been injured and have hired me to find them a post-accident home. As your REALTOR®, I need to work closely with you and your family, your case manager, occupational therapist (OT), lawyer, and home modification expert. Collectively, the goal is to ensure you can be discharged from the hospital or rehab centre to a home that will meet your mobility needs, is comfortable and is within your budget.

A list of housing needs and wants is compiled based on input from you and your rehab team. My job is to research all available options and present them to you. If renovations to the home are required to make it accessible, the home modification expert needs to prepare a renovation plan and estimate. Bank financing or insurance funding will need to be coordinated. And your OT needs to confirm that the living space and modifications will work for you before a final decision is made.

Most accessible homes (houses and condominiums) are modified for a specific person. And usually, that person lives there for a long time. For that reason, accessible homes do not come on the market very often.

You'll most likely need to buy a home that can be modified to suit your specific needs.

Which Option Is Best For You?

House

If you've got a large family that requires a lot of space, then buying a house might make sense. Single-level bungalows are often ideal, but residential elevators and Telecabs can make two-story houses accessible for everyone. But remember that not all houses are suitable to modify. For example, side splits and back splits often have too many stairs, and townhouses can be too narrow to install an elevator.

This telecab was added to give easy access to the second floor

Condominium

There are many advantages to purchasing a condominium. For example, the maintenance of the building and grounds are included in condo fees and handled by outside contractors.

Renovations, however, may not be as easy to make in a condo unit. Plumbing can be a particular challenge since toilet drains and main water lines cannot be moved, and this has to be factored into any renovations that are required.

Accessibility throughout the whole building must also be considered. The entrance, parking area, and amenity areas all need to be looked at. Automatic door openers are also critical. And can the underground parking garage accommodate the height of your vehicle, provide transfer space and an accessible path to enter the building?

Rental

Over the past two years, there have been several new rental buildings that have been built across Canada. Most of these new buildings have select suites with larger washrooms that feature a 5-foot turning radius and wider doors, but despite the demand, these new buildings don't have suites with roll-in showers. Unfortunately, rental suites with a roll-in shower are extremely rare and it requires a very focused search to find one.

Short-Term-Stay Accessible Hotel

Many newer hotels have one- and two-bedroom suites with roll-in showers. This can be a very good option in the short term; however, it can be very costly over the long term.

Quick Decision

There is a lot to consider and often time is limited to find suitable housing after a traumatic accident, and quick decisions are often needed. Planning for housing has to begin as soon as is practical after your accident.

CHAPTER 15
FINDING THE PERFECT HOME TO RENOVATE

If you currently live in a home that has been modified for your accessibility needs, there is a strong likelihood you're not moving anytime soon. If you're a buyer wanting to purchase a barrier-free home, you may need to wait a long time for the right home to become available. This is especially true if you're looking for a specific type of home, configuration or price point, or you want to be in a specific neighbourhood.

For these reasons, you might choose to do what the majority of my clients have done and buy a home you can renovate to your specific needs and dreams. However, before you make a move, there are lots of things to consider when evaluating a house or condominium and the neighbourhood it's located in.

Location, Location, Location!

Everyone is familiar with the real estate adage "Location, location, location." The perfect home cannot score a 10/10 unless the neighbourhood suits your needs as well.

Make a list of the amenities you absolutely need and the ones you simply want. Local transit, library, grocery stores, pharmacies, medical clinics, schools, parks and places of worship are just a few examples.

Now prioritize the items on that list to determine which ones you really do need to make the location the right one. And remember, even if all of the amenities are close by, you may also have to assess the level of accessibility for each. A feature as simple as a curb cut or a ramp can make all the difference in the world. But unfortunately, not all buildings will be accessible, especially if they are more than a few years old. For instance, an older church or library may welcome you with steps leading to the entrance.

Looking for a House?

Look for a home that has the potential to meet your long-term needs. Allow for family growth and aging, taking into consideration both functional and spatial needs that you may require in the future. Buying a home with a bit more space can be far more cost-effective than building an addition in the future.

Ideally, look for a home that has an attached two-car garage. This will allow room for parking and direct access into the home via a ramp or mechanical lift – a definite benefit in inclement weather.

This house was modified to add a main floor bedroom and ensuite bathroom along with a mechanical lift from the garage to the main floor

This home was custom built to be accessible

This home was modified to become accessible

An open-concept bungalow-style home is ideal for many. A kitchen with a view of the family room is a bonus when friends and family are visiting. But having said that, don't rule out a two-story home with an elevating device. A two-story home can actually offer more square footage for a comparable price once you factor in the cost to build and land values.

Purchasing a Condo?

The condo building itself must be accessible, including common areas that are used by everyone in the family. Consider the entrance, social spaces and recreation facilities. The carpeting in the lobby may look nice but makes it harder to navigate with a wheelchair. The underground parking will need to accommodate the height of your vehicle, transfer space, and include an accessible path to enter the building. And don't forget to consider the ease of using the access pass cards or key fobs to enter underground parking, unlock doors and operate elevators.

Plumbing is very difficult and expensive to relocate in a condo. Ensure the washroom has adequate space or room for expansion while maintaining all drains as they currently exist, especially the 4-inch toilet drain.

The bathtub was removed and replaced with a roll in shower

Talk with the building manager to gauge the willingness of the condo board to approve in-suite modifications. For example, removing a bathtub and replacing it with a roll-in shower will require the approval of the condo board. And adding an automatic opener to your suite door requires altering the lock on the hallway side of the door which is considered a common area and therefore would also need board approval.

If you're concerned with getting out of the building in an emergency, consider purchasing a unit below the seventh floor with a balcony situated over a fire route. This will allow a fire department aerial ladder to reach you. You can also purchase an evacuation chair (www.Evacuscape.com) that you can transfer onto and a second person can safely push you down the stairs. And always register your evacuation plan with the local fire department, so in an emergency, they'll know which stairwell and level to send help to.

Plan Ahead

Regardless of what you buy or where you buy, the most important thing you can do is plan ahead. Look ahead 5 years, 10 years and longer. Will your new home meet your current needs and future needs? Can your home grow and adapt with you? Enlist the advice of an OT to help you answer these questions.

Investment Opportunity

There is considerable demand for barrier-free rental properties across Canada, but there is very little inventory. As I mentioned in Chapter 14, finding a rental property with a roll-in shower is very rare. This is an opportunity for a savvy investor.

In addition to the 6 million Canadians who are living with a disability, there is a demand for barrier-free rentals from:

- People recovering from surgery
- Those who have been injured in an accident and are being discharged from a hospital or rehab centre
- Older adults who are downsizing or want to age in place

Demand exceeds supply. If you're looking for an investment opportunity, the time is right to invest in a barrier-free rental property.

CHAPTER 16
THE CANADIAN HOME BUILDERS ASSOCIATION'S HOME MODIFICATION COUNCIL

If you love where you live, and want to continue to safely and successfully live there, you'll probably need to make at least one or two of the modifications discussed in this book. To do that, you'll need to find a contractor who has the necessary expertise and experience. The Canadian Home Builders Association (CHBA) can help.

Canadian
Home Builders'
Association

The Canadian Home Builders' Association Logo

The CHBA has recognized the importance and the need for home modifications across Canada by creating the Home Modification Council. The Mission Statement of the CHBA clearly identifies their mandate to ensure "Canadians of all ages and life stages can choose the type of home and location best suited to their needs." An important element of the group includes connecting people who want to safely remain in their own homes with:

- Accurate and relevant information about home modifications
- Qualified contractors
- Professionals, including health care professionals who support home modifications

CHBA's Home Modification Council (HMC) provides much-needed coordination, connecting the consumer with those who have the expertise, appropriate resources, and needed services to make it possible to live at home successfully for people with disabilities and older adults.

Gary Sharp is the Director of Renovations with the Canadian Home Builders Association. He is very enthusiastic about the HMC: "Home modifications allowing Canadians with disabilities and Canada's seniors to age in place is a very specific and important subset of the renovation industry. The HMC has the opportunity to make a positive contribution to help people live independently. For family caregivers who often find themselves in a position where home modifications must be made quickly, the HMC will be a source of information and provide caregivers with a way to find trained and knowledgeable contractors. This will help to reduce the stress of renovating, allow for the appropriate work to be completed, and improve quality of life for those needing home modifications."

More details are available on the CHBA website: **www.CHBA.ca**

CHAPTER 17
THE UK LEADS THE WAY

One of the biggest challenges to making home modifications a reality for Canadians is funding.

According to a March of Dimes Canada study, the average cost to modify a home is $8 a day. Yes, you're reading that correctly! This is the average home modification cost amortized over the lifetime of the renovation. Even though this is an affordable amount, there is very limited funding available in Canada to modify homes.

The United Kingdom (UK) has addressed the funding question, and I think it's a model that Canada should look at closely. I recently attended a presentation by Paul Smith, the Director of Foundations in the United Kingdom. Paul traveled to Ontario to share his insights on home adaptations (modifications) in England.

Foundations is a government organization that oversees a national network of Home Improvement Agencies (HIAs) across England. Foundations uses a collaborative approach to make connections between the public, private and academic sectors with the goal to effect change. The fact that Paul travelled "across the pond" to share his expertise and experiences working in the UK with the pioneers of the home modification industry in Canada speaks volumes about his dedication to this field.

In the UK, people with disabilities can apply to their local HIA for a grant called "Disabled Facilities Grants" or DFGs, to pay for home modifications.

A bathroom in the UK that was modified with a
Disabled Facilities Grant

HIAs are located throughout the UK and have a mandate to ensure people are able to stay safe, secure, and warm and remain independent in their own home. To achieve their mandate, they provide grant money to people with a permanent physical disability, learning disability, sensory impairment or mental illness.

You're Legally Entitled to Funding

In the UK, homeowners and tenants have a statutory (legal) right to receive grant money to adapt their homes. Paul told me that the UK Government invests £500,000,000 per year (approx. $854,000,000 CDN) in the program and it's based on a simple business case: "If you're disabled, you're much more likely to remain in your own home if it's properly adapted. The alternative of moving into care is something no one wants and costs far more for the individual and the state."

Grants can be used to pay for:

- Ramps
- Stairlifts
- Through floor lifts
- Ceiling tracks
- Wider doors
- Wet room (bathroom) with zero-threshold shower
- Accessible toilet
- Accessible kitchen
- Improved heating
- Accessible controls
- Safety features

How It Works

When a person first contacts their local HIA, an occupational therapist is assigned to the file and comes to their home for an assessment. Based on that assessment, the OT will make home modification recommendations.

The grant is means-tested – tied to income – and Paul told me it's a relatively complex calculation. The maximum grant is £30,000 (about $52,000 CDN), and the average grant is approximately £8,000 (about $13,900 CDN).

Both homeowners and tenants can apply. And you must agree to stay living in the modified home for at least 5 years. Approximately 40 percent of applicants are tenants, and 60 percent are homeowners.

The UK model for organizing and funding home modifications is impressive for a number of reasons. First, the UK government has acknowledged the benefit, both economically and socially, to having older adults and people with disabilities stay in their homes and the community.

Second, having an established network of home modification contractors is crucial.

And third, the involvement of an OT at the start of the process ensures that homeowners and tenants are being given proper advice.

For more information on home modifications in the United Kingdom, Foundations or Disabled Facilities Grants, you can visit the following websites:

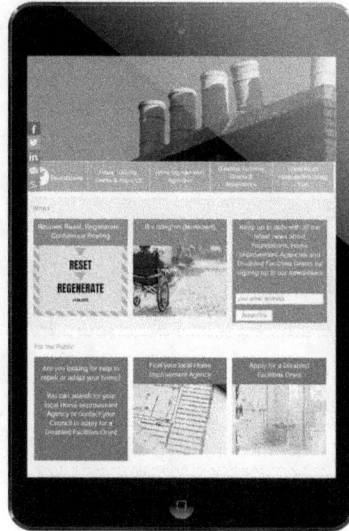

www.AdaptMyHome.org.uk   www.Foundations.uk.com

Here in Canada, we can learn a great deal from the UK model. Funding for home modifications needs to be a priority.

CHAPTER 18
ACCESSIBILITY DESIGNED PROGRAM

Over the years, options for accessible, barrier-free homes and condominiums have grown, but nothing to date has compared to the Daniels Corporation's Accessibility Designed Program.

It's been over 20 years since I can recall a condo builder offering standardized plans that are designed to be accessible right from the start (see the story of my aunt's condo in the introduction.) Historically if a buyer wanted a new condo with a roll-in shower, accessible kitchen, and other features, they had to find a builder willing to customize their plans, often resulting in substantial additional costs.

Daniels is offering preconstruction condos with the following features at *no additional cost*:

- The bathroom will include:
  - Roll-in shower with grab bars
  - Under-sink clearance
  - Transfer space beside the toilet
  - 59-inch (1500 mm) turning radius
- Roll-out balcony with swing door

- Rough-in for power-operated entry door
- Minimum 34-inch (860 mm) doors throughout

Artist's rendering of the Daniels ADP bathroom

Daniels is also offering an upgraded alternative kitchen plan that includes:

- Lowered counter height of 34 inches (860 mm)
- Roll-under sink and cooktop
- Side-opening oven
- Dishwasher drawer
- Double-door fridge

Artist's rendering of the Daniels ADP kitchen

As a REALTOR®, I represent several buyers that have purchased ADP suites and my buyers are looking forward to moving into their new condos as the buildings are completed. I've created a website to keep you up to date on this initiative: **www.AccessibilityDesigned.com**

The Accessibility Designed Program (ADP) suites have been a great success and Daniels has committed to including ADP suites of their new communities. I'm confident that other builders across Canada will take notice and follow Daniels' lead.

CHAPTER 19
FLEXHOUSING™
AND CO-HOUSING

FlexHousing™ and co-housing are two very different concepts, but they both offer significant opportunities for people with disabilities and older adults looking to age in place.

FlexHousing™

FlexHousing™ is a trademarked innovation of the Canada Mortgage and Housing Corporation (CMHC). Its approach to home design, renovation and construction is based on adaptability and accessibility. The home's design can adapt to the changing needs of your family and the concepts can be integrated seamlessly within all forms of conventional housing, including single-family homes, duplexes and multi-unit residential buildings.

The floor plan and layout of a FlexHome™ will have built-in features that allow you to easily change the available space as needed or preferred at a future date. Plumbing and wiring are roughed in wherever possible – over the garage, in the basement and in the attic – and left for finishing later to accommodate changing needs.

Planned adaptability means interior spaces are easily converted. For instance, a main floor two-piece washroom can easily become a three-piece bathroom with the addition of a shower stall. Or a main floor study can become a bedroom. Or a large room can be easily divided into two rooms thanks to the initial design that included two doors, two closets, two windows and two light fixtures with separate switches.

Other examples include:

- A second-story room that was prewired and preplumbed so that it can be easily converted into a kitchen should there be a need to divide the house into two units.

- Bathrooms built with reinforced walls to support future grab bars, adequate transfer space to toilet, no-threshold shower with adjustable-height showerhead.

- Stair access to the second floor has no curves, landings or changes in direction to accommodate the installation of a stairlift or inclined platform lift at a future time.

- Adequate height in the attic to convert to future living space if required.

There are many benefits to a house built with the FlexHousing™ concepts:

- Young families can benefit by reconfiguring rooms to meet their changing spatial requirements over time.

- Those who want to age in place or persons with disabilities will not have to undertake expensive renovations since accessibility and barrier-free design have already been planned.

- Homeowners who no longer need as much space, or those seeking rental income opportunities can change the configuration from a larger home to two smaller units.

Renovations become much simpler to meet the needs of a growing family, persons with disabilities or an individual wanting to age in place. You can download a copy of CMHC's FlexHousing™ Pocket Planner on the CMHC website at: **www.CMHC.ca**

Co-Housing

There are two distinct models of co-housing. The first is a community of individual self-contained homes clustered around a central common area and amenities. A number of these communities are already established across Canada, and more are in development. The Canadian Cohousing Network's website has a lot of information on these communities: **www.Cohousing.ca**

The second model is based on a single home with shared ownership. The premise for this type of co-housing is non-related individuals live in the same home and share housing expenses and household amenities.

I started writing about the shared ownership model of co-housing in 2014. Since then, the concept has gained in popularity among these groups:

- Older adults looking to age in place with other like-minded people
- Multigenerational families

- Young adults who pool their finances to purchase a home

I see a lot of potential with the co-housing model if it were to be integrated with barrier-free properties. I have seen many instances where young people with disabilities have to live in assisted living facilities where the residents are almost all seniors. Co-housing could provide all of the benefits of assisted living while still providing independence along with the benefit of homeownership. Individuals could share in the cost of attendant care services, housekeeping, grass cutting, etc.

There can be a lot of flexibility in the shared ownership co-housing model. For instance, there is no set figure for the number of potential owners. And owners could be individuals or couples.

Co-owners would have the advantage of sharing the common expenses while still ensuring they have their own private living space. For instance, every owner could have their own unique suite providing a bedroom, bathroom, storage area and individual temperature controls. Each private bathroom could be barrier-free and include a roll-in shower, roll-under vanity and grab bars. And the house could feature spacious accessible common areas including kitchen, dining and living rooms.

The individuals would be tenants in common – each owning an undivided interest in the home – providing each owner with a long-term real estate investment. Co-owners would own an interest in the whole property, not just their exclusive-use area.

In a traditional assisted living situation, the facility is responsible for overseeing all of the attendant caregivers. In a co-housing arrangement, the owners would control and together share in the decisions and costs around hiring and managing care.

Co-housing offers the advantages of community living and shared resources while still providing personal privacy and independence. And as an owner, you maintain total control over your finances and your personal living space.

As people look for new, innovative and safe housing options, FlexHousing™ and co-housing will continue to gain in popularity in the coming years.

CHAPTER 20
FINANCING OPTIONS FOR HOME MODIFICATIONS

Over the years, most of my clients have chosen to make modifications to their homes. While the scope of work may be different for each client, what most of them have in common is the need to arrange financing to pay for the work.

When making any financial decision, it is important to get accurate information from the experts such as a mortgage broker or your financial advisor. They can explain the best products on the market, help you understand your options, and provide guidance on how much you can borrow. Don't make a decision involving the equity you have in your home, only to find out later that there were better options available to you.

Banks have a variety of options to choose from – ranging from financing for small amounts of money – maybe you need to install a ramp, handrail or widen a doorway – to larger amounts for bigger projects such as a barrier-free kitchen and bathroom. Will you need all the money upfront or will the work be done in stages, requiring cash flow as the renovations progress?

Suggested Guidelines

- A small renovation under $5,000 may be best suited to your credit card provided you can pay the balance off each month.

- Expenses between $10,000 and $20,000 may be better suited to a credit line. With some credit lines, you only pay interest on the amount borrowed.

- For projects over $20,000 you might consider refinancing your mortgage for the amount required.

Reverse mortgages are also an option for those 55+. A reverse mortgage is a simple way to access funds that would otherwise stay locked in the equity of your home.

The benefit of a reversible mortgage is that the lender pays you, instead of you paying the lender. Whether you choose to receive a portion of your home's value in monthly payments, a lump sum, or in the form of credit you can access as needed, you can improve your standard of living by turning part of your home's value into tax-free cash. The best part of a reverse mortgage is you can defer re-payment until you sell your home.

Always do your homework and make these decisions in consultation with a professional. Look at all of the options and the costs involved now and down the road.

The Canada Mortgage and Housing Corporation (CMHC) suggests you set aside a percentage of your renovation funds to cover items you may not have considered in the work you are planning. For instance, you may realize you need to upgrade additional features in your home that you had not originally thought of. A little money set aside will reduce the need to renegotiate your financial arrangements.

Planning ahead to ensure your home modification design meets your current and long-term needs is vital. And with a detailed design budget, you can ensure adequate financing which will help reduce some of the stress that usually accompanies a home modification project.

CHAPTER 21
A PRACTICAL GUIDE TO DOWNSIZING

At some point in your life, you'll probably be faced with the need to downsize, move or help prepare a home for sale.

Ideally, it'll be at a time when you're healthy and simply realize that it is time to live a simpler life with less stress. Or it may be at a time, as many caregivers of older persons have discovered, you're needing to face the challenge of moving a loved one from the home they have lived in for decades, to a smaller more manageable home or one that offers assistance with daily activities.

There are many reasons for moving, including:

- The home has become too much work to maintain

- The desire to reduce expenses

- A need for the income from the sale of the family home to continue to live comfortably

- Living closer to local amenities and public transportation makes more sense

- It's time to move to an accessible home

- Living closer to other family members

Hiring Help

Whatever the case, the process can be difficult, and although there is no way to make it pain-free, there are a variety of professionals you can hire and steps you can take to reduce the stress.

If you have the luxury of being able to afford some help, there are excellent companies that provide specialized services for any situation you may find yourself in. Here is a list of professional services you can call on to help with the downsizing process:

- Appraiser
- Auctioneer
- Charities that pick up
- Decluttering specialist
- Downsizing expert
- Estate lawyer
- Financial planner
- Handyman
- Home organizer
- Home renovator
- Haul-away service
- Moving company

The experts know what to do and how to do it, they know the answers to your questions, and they can commit the time needed to handle the job that seems overwhelming to you. Although the services may vary, the experts can provide the specific assistance needed to save you some of the physical and emotional stress, including:

- Developing a plan designed specifically for your situation
- Actually sorting, selling, and packing your belongings
- Preparing your home for sale, including cleaning, painting and staging
- Moving and setting up what you are taking to the new home
- Unpacking and helping to get you settled
- Managing an estate sale
- Special services that are unique to your needs

Doing It Yourself

If calling in the professionals to do the work for you is not an option, there is no choice but to get started.

Some people like to take photos of every room, scanning from one corner to the next to capture everything. Photos can remind you later why you did not keep a lot of the contents; it will also give you a snapshot of the place your family called home.

Take the time to write down special memories or any family history that is connected to special items. This information will be cherished for generations to come and will contribute to the value of family heirlooms. The photos and the family history will make great memories for a digital album.

Starting with the garbage is the easiest step: throw out anything that has no value to anyone else. But remember, many charities are now running thrift shops, selling what would have been thrown in the garbage in the past. A good thrift shop can recycle and keep a lot of items from going to landfill sites. But if you do actually have to collect up garbage, have a plan to get the bags and boxes to the dump.

Consider what you will do with everything. The most common sorting options are:

- Articles you will put in a garage sale

- Clothes, household items and furniture that can go to charity (and plan ahead so you have a charity that will pick everything up on a designated day)

- Items you might sell on Kijiji, Craigslist, through a classified ad or through an auctioneer

- Items that can be used by – or have been promised to – family members.

Identify the items that you want to keep for use in the new home, but be realistic about the space you will have.

Keep the items that are most important to you and that you cannot live without. Don't be surprised if you change your mind often.

If you or your parents are still living in the home, start with the rooms that have been used the least over the recent years – extra bedrooms, upstairs storage areas, the basement, and dining room. Start the sorting and clearing process in these rooms because it will be least disruptive to everyday life.

By starting in the rooms least used, you will likely find items that have not been used in a considerable length of time and that will not be missed when passed on to children, grandchildren, charity or the auction house. Start making a list of the items you know will be wanted by someone in the family. Label them.

Start With the Big Stuff

Begin with the large items in each room and work your way down to the small items. It's easier to start with furniture and the bigger pieces and you'll feel like you are making some progress. If you start with the small items, you may get overwhelmed and frustrated before you even get started.

Create a System

Have a sorting system. Sort items by using stickers, making piles, or making detailed lists of what will be kept, what will be given away and to where, and what is still undecided.

Agree on a system. Create a clear system for identifying who gets what to avoid disagreements among adult children and other family members.

Be sure everyone gets something special or meaningful. Be prepared for disagreements, but remember it is likely an emotional time for everyone in the family. Stay calm and encourage negotiation. The value of an item may be financial or sentimental.

Mark items that might be useful for grandchildren who are setting up residence in university or their own homes.

Identify items of value that should be appraised before you decide what to do with them. You can often hire a service agency to catalog and appraise your possessions and coordinate a home auction for a percentage of the profit.

Give it Away Now

If you are the one downsizing, consider bequeathing items now. Identify those items you want certain family members to have and consider what items you are willing to share now. Remember, you may get more pleasure out of seeing your granddaughter enjoy your china at the next family event than knowing she will have it after you are gone.

Get rid of things you no longer need. Be realistic about what items you use regularly and what items you are just used to having around. The electric carving knife you use at Thanksgiving may not be as necessary as the toaster oven you use every morning.

Ask yourself some questions when you can't decide what to purge:

- When did I use it or wear it last?
- Can another item serve the same purpose?
- Does the item have sentimental value?
- What shape is it in?
- Could someone else use it and/or need it more than I do?
- Do I really need it?

Charity

If you are donating to charity, you may be eligible for a tax-deductible receipt. Consider thinking of specific organizations for specific items. For example, donating your professional wardrobe to an abused women's shelter or employment assistance program; donating books to the local library sale; offering furniture to the Red Cross for fire victims; giving old instruments to a school music program, or a box of teacups and saucers to a local group or seniors home that holds a 'Mother's Day tea.'

Kids' Stuff

Have the kids come and get the stuff that you have been storing for them for years. There comes a time for them to store their own childhood mementos – although many parents admit to still having a couple of boxes of hockey cards, comic books and action figures! Give them a deadline that works with your schedule and warn them that anything left over will be donated to charity. You may be surprised that they are suddenly ready to part with their belongings.

Have a Schedule

Work in scheduled blocks of time. The process of revisiting memories and making decisions about items you have lived with for many years can be emotionally difficult. You will feel less overwhelmed and make better decisions if you take regular breaks and allow yourself time to digest what is happening.

Storage Units

You may be tempted to rent a storage unit – many people do. But that only delays the inevitable. Staff at a rental unit I visited once said that the rented space helps alleviate the guilt of getting rid of family possessions, but out of sight is out of mind. Eventually, the boxes and furniture get purged, sometimes after years of paying a rental fee.

You Can Do It!

Leaving a family home can be a bittersweet event that involves revisiting many memories. During the process of downsizing you may be surprised at how attached you have become to some possessions and how difficult it might seem to part with them. It is important to remember, however, that it is the relationships in our lives that give us the most pleasure. A life filled with possessions is no compensation for a life filled with family, friends, and meaningful connections.

20 Tips to Make Moving and Downsizing Stress-Free – or as Stress-Free as Possible!

- Whenever possible, plan ahead for the inevitable day that you need to downsize your own or your parent's home.

- Consider all the options on where to move to, comparing costs, services, waiting lists and the match between what they offer and what you need.

- Identify the community resources that are available to help.

- Decide if you want to do it all yourself or hire the experts.

- Start with the items that truly have no value to anyone else.

- Take photos.

- Record some family history.

- Sort items that can be sold.

- Identify what you need to take to your new home.

- Start in the rooms that are used the least in the house.

- Sort the large items first, then smaller ones; or work on one room at a time.

- Agree on a system with your siblings and other family members on how to divide up the things they want to keep.

- Make a list of what is going where.

- Ask the kids to come and get the stuff you have been storing for them.

- Work in blocks of time; remember to take regular breaks.

- Take some time to let the memories come to the surface; some laughing, some crying and shedding tears are normal.

- Rent storage space – but only as a last resort.

- Accept that change is not easy for anyone.

- Recognize and allow yourself time to go through the emotional roller coaster that many people experience.

- All my clients have to downsize or at least purge to a certain degree before moving. This handy checklist can help you make a game plan to downsize efficiently.

CONCLUSION

Everyone benefits from an accessible home regardless of age or ability.

Often simple changes can make all of the difference between being independent and dependent in your own home. An entrance solution, bathroom solution, a well-designed kitchen, an accessible home office, and an enabled garden are all examples of the modifications you can make. Combined with the innovations in home design, smart home technology, home care technology and assistive devices, living safely and independently at home is achievable.

Outside your home, Canadian local, provincial, and federal governments are supporting initiatives and legislation to make our cities and communities more accessible.

Whether you're one of the 6 million Canadians with a disability, one of the 8.5 million family caregivers across the country, or part of the 85% of older adults who want to age in place, achieving freedom at home is now more important than ever and it starts with planning ahead!

Custom home, built to be fully accessible

ABOUT THE AUTHOR

Jeffrey Kerr is a REALTOR® with RE/MAX Unique Inc. Brokerage, in Toronto, Ontario, Canada. He earned his real estate Licence in 1999 and his Broker's licence in 2007. In 2019 he received the RE/MAX Lifetime Achievement Award. He has both the Senior Real Estate Specialist and Accredited Senior Agent designations. Jeffrey is the go-to real estate agent for buyers and sellers of barrier free, accessible homes.

Jeffrey lives in Toronto with his wife and three children. He enjoys playing squash, tennis and skiing and is an enthusiastic Blue Jays baseball fan.

www.ingramcontent.com/pod-product-compliance
Lightning Source LLC
Chambersburg PA
CBHW060135100426
42744CB00007B/791

* 9 7 8 1 9 8 9 2 0 3 0 9 5 *